S0-ADP-056

heavenly
chocolate

heavenly
chocolate

RYLAND
PETERS
& SMALL
LONDON NEW YORK

linda collister
photography by **debi treloar**

To my recipe tasters—Emily, Danny, and Stevie

Designer	Luis Peral-Aranda
Commissioning Editor	Elsa Petersen-Schepelern
Production	Deborah Wehner
Art Director	Gabriella Le Grazie
Publishing Director	Alison Starling
Food Stylist	Linda Collister
Stylist	Helen Trent
Photographer's Assistant	Lina Ikse Bergman

Author's acknowledgments

I would like to thank the following for their help with this book:

Elsa Petersen-Schepelern, Luis Peral-Aranda, Debi Treloar, Barbara Levy, Helen Trent, Annette and Will Hertz,

Alan and Simon Silverwood of Alan Silverwood Ltd for loaf pans and baking sheets. And last but certainly not least Alan Hertz.

ISBN 1 84172 211 1

Printed and bound in China

First published in the United States in 2001
by Ryland Peters & Small, Inc.
519 Broadway, 5th Floor
New York, NY 10012
www.rylandpeters.com

10 9 8 7 6 5 4 3 2 1

Text © Linda Collister 2001

Design and photographs © Ryland Peters & Small 2001

Notes

All spoon measurements are level unless otherwise stated.

Before baking, weigh or measure all ingredients exactly and prepare baking pans or sheets.

Make sure your oven has reached the correct temperature before putting in the recipe to be baked—use an oven thermometer to check the thermostat is working properly. Every oven is different, so the baking times can only be guidelines. Recipes in this book were tested in four different kinds of ovens—all work slightly differently. Consult the maker's handbook for special instructions.

Some recipes contain raw or lightly cooked eggs. Because of the risk of transmitting salmonella, these recipes should not be eaten by the elderly, young children, pregnant women, or those with reduced immune systems.

contents

6   heavenly chocolate ...

10   sweet treats

16   chocolate confections

42   chocolate desserts

54   chocolate sauces

58   chocolate drinks

64   index

heavenly chocolate ...

Once, chocolate was thought of as a stimulant and medicine, a cure for hangovers and a source of strength and energy. It was Queen Anne's doctor in the early 18th century who thought of adding milk and feeding it to her sickly children. He eventually sold the recipe to the Quakers, who saw the drink as a healthy alternative to alcohol. Chocolate is now known to contain phosphorous, iron, calcium, and theobromine which affects the central nervous system and acts as an anti-depressant, so no wonder it makes us feel good.

These days, chocolate is a rare indulgence for me, as I struggle to eat a balanced diet, but I find the principle of "a little of what you fancy does you good" actually works: a little top-quality chocolate really hits the spot in a way that cheap, sweet, fatty chocolate candy bars do not. I get a great kick out of a slice of warm chocolate torte on my birthday, because it is such a special treat, and my taste buds are not jaded.

Using the best ingredients will really make a difference to the taste and quality of any recipe you make. Choose the finest chocolate you can afford, and look out for the organic brands.

Choosing chocolate

The most important rule—read the label before you buy. The best chocolate is made from a blend of beans, rather like coffee, and the flavor depends on the beans used, plus the proportion of cocoa solids and cocoa butter, plus sugar and flavorings. For best taste and final results, choose dark, plain chocolate with cocoa solids around 70 percent, and pure vanilla extract. Most supermarkets carry Lindt, Ghiradelli, and own-brand, high-quality, plain chocolate at fair prices. Plain chocolate with less than 50 percent cocoa solids will taste very sweet and destroy the flavor of your recipe. It will usually include synthetic flavors and vegetable oils rather than cocoa butter. Avoid very cheap cake covering blocks: they are mostly sugar and vegetable fats. White chocolate does not contain cocoa solids but is made from cocoa butter, sugar, and milk solids: avoid cheap white chocolate candy, as it will taste greasy and sweet. Milk chocolate uses milk solids instead of some of the cocoa solids, so look out for brands with a high cocoa solid content and pure vanilla.

Storing chocolate

Store chocolate away from other foods in a cool, dry spot. Avoid storing in the fridge or below 55°F, as beads of moisture will form as it returns to room temperature. Working with chocolate is tricky in hot, humid weather or in a steamy kitchen, so try to work when it's cool.

Chopping and grating

In most recipes, chocolate is grated or chopped. In warm weather, chill the chocolate until firm before you start, then use the large-hole side of the grater for grating. Use a clean, dry board and a large knife for chopping. Chocolate can also be chopped in a processor using the pulse button—take care not to overwork the chocolate or it can turn warm and sticky. When chopping chocolate for melting, it's important that the chocolate is cut into evenly sized pieces, so it all melts at the same rate.

Melting chocolate

Chocolate starts to melt at about 86°F (that's why it melts in the mouth), and burns at 230°F. For best results, melt it slowly and gradually, as it easily becomes overheated and scorched and turns into an unusable solid lump. Set the chopped chocolate in a heatproof bowl set over a saucepan of steaming hot but not boiling water. The water must not touch the base of the bowl and don't let a drop of water or steam reach the chocolate or it will seize up. Don't cover the bowl for the same reason. Stir gently and remove the bowl from the heat as soon as the chocolate has melted. If chocolate becomes overheated, and turns into a heavy, rough lump, remove the bowl from the heat and stir in warm vegetable oil, a teaspoon at a time, until smooth again.

Microwaving

Chocolate can also be melted in the microwave, but it should be completely dry inside before you start. It's best to consult the handbook first, but I use the lowest setting and stir and check the progress of the chocolate every minute. It will take less time when melted with butter or a liquid.

sweet treats

christmas prunes

Extra-large pitted prunes (the biggest you can find) are soaked in brandy or rum then stuffed with marzipan and coated with dark chocolate—try them with coffee after dinner. They make a delicious gift, packaged in pretty boxes.

Arrange the prunes in a single layer in a shallow dish. Ease them open, then spoon the brandy or rum into the cavity inside each prune so they are well lubricated. Cover and let soak for several hours or overnight.

Divide the marzipan into 12 equal pieces. Using your hands, roll each to a small egg shape, big enough to fill the cavity in the prune. Put a piece of shaped marzipan inside each prune, molding the prune back into its original form. Set on the lined tray.

Gently melt the chocolate in a heatproof bowl set over a saucepan of steaming but not boiling water. Remove the bowl from the pan and stir gently. Let cool until thickened and almost setting. Using a teaspoon, pour chocolate over each prune to coat—don't worry if they are not perfect as they will look more attractive. Leave in a cool place, but not the refrigerator if possible, until set, then remove from the paper. Store in an airtight container somewhere cool. Best within 5 days.

12 large, pitted prunes
3 tablespoons brandy or dark rum
4 oz. marzipan
3½ oz. bittersweet chocolate, finely chopped

a tray, lined with parchment paper or wax paper

Makes 12

chocolate truffles

Wrap in paper bags and tie with a gorgeous ribbon for an irresistible gift! Truffles are a popular Christmas treat in France and the possibilities for variations are huge—there's even a white truffle.

⅞ cup heavy cream

10½ oz. bittersweet chocolate, finely chopped

To coat

9 oz. bittersweet chocolate, chopped

good ½ cup finest quality unsweetened cocoa, sifted

several trays lined with parchment paper or wax paper

a piping bag with ½-inch plain nozzle

Makes 50

Put the cream in a saucepan, gently bring to a boil, then remove from the heat and cool for a minute. Put the chopped chocolate into a heatproof bowl and pour on the hot cream, gently stir a couple of times until smooth, then let cool.

When the mixture is cold but not set, beat vigorously with a wooden spoon until very thick and lighter in color and texture. Using a teaspoon or piping bag, set marble-sized pieces of the mixture onto the prepared trays. You can also roll the mixture into balls with your hands. Chill until very firm.

When ready to finish the truffles, put the remaining chocolate in a heatproof bowl set over a saucepan of steaming but not boiling water and melt gently. Remove from the heat and stir until smooth. Leave until cool.

Using 2 forks, briefly dip each truffle in the chocolate until coated. Return the coated truffles to the lined trays and leave until the coating chocolate is almost set (if the truffles are very cold this might be immediate), then roll in the cocoa. Pack into small boxes and chill. Store in the refrigerator for up to 1 week. Eat at room temperature.

Variations:

Snowball Truffles Coat the chilled truffles in melted white chocolate, then roll in unsweetened shredded coconut (optional).

Rum or Brandy Truffles Add 3 tablespoons dark rum or brandy to the chocolate, then add the cream and continue as in the main recipe.

Drambuie or Tia Maria Truffles Add 2 tablespoons Drambuie or Tia Maria as above.

Cherry Liqueur Truffles Add 2 tablespoons syrup from a jar of Morello cherries in Kirsch. Halve cherries if large and drain well on paper towels. Push a half into the center of each shaped truffle and enclose. Let set, then coat and finish.

chocolate fudge

A quick and easy recipe with a rich flavor.

Put the chocolate and butter in a large heatproof bowl set over a saucepan of steaming but not boiling water. Melt gently. Remove the bowl from the pan and gently stir in the cream, then the vanilla or rum, followed by the corn syrup.

Using a wooden spoon, then your hands, work in the confectioners' sugar, 1 tablespoon at a time, to make a thick, smooth fudge. If the mixture starts to stiffen before all the sugar has been incorporated, return the bowl to the heat for a minute or so.

Turn the mixture into the prepared pan and press in evenly. Chill until firm, then turn out and cut into squares with a large sharp knife. Store up to 10 days in the refrigerator.

3½ oz. bittersweet chocolate, finely chopped

4 tablespoons unsalted butter

2 tablespoons heavy cream

1 teaspoon vanilla extract or dark rum

1 tablespoon corn syrup

scant 2 cups confectioners' sugar, sifted

a shallow, 8-inch square pan, buttered

Makes 20 squares

nut fudge

Cut the fudge into squares and store in the refrigerator.

1 stick unsalted butter

1 cup unsweetened cocoa, sifted

6 oz. can evaporated milk

3⅞ cups confectioners' sugar, sifted

¾ cup walnut pieces or toasted hazelnuts

a shallow, 8-inch square pan, buttered

a candy thermometer

Makes 20 squares

Put the butter in a large, heavy saucepan, melt gently, then remove from the heat and stir in the unsweetened cocoa powder, evaporated milk, and, finally, the sugar. Set the pan over low heat and stir constantly until the mixture comes to a boil. Boil gently, stirring frequently to avoid the mixture catching on the bottom of the pan, until the mixture reaches "soft ball" stage, that is when a candy thermometer reads 240°F or when a little of the fudge dropped from a spoon into a bowl of cold water forms a soft, moldable ball. This will take about 25 minutes and the mixture will bubble up, so take care.

Remove the pan from the heat, stir in the nuts, pour into the prepared pan, and press in evenly with the back of a spoon. Chill until almost set, then mark into squares, cover, and chill until firm. Store up to 10 days in the refrigerator.

chocolate
confections

bûche de noël–yule log

Vanilla sponge

4 large eggs, room temperature

a heaping ⅓ cup sugar

½ teaspoon vanilla extract

1 cup all-purpose flour

a good pinch of salt

3 tablespoons unsalted butter, melted and cooled

Ganache

¾ cup heavy cream

7 oz. bittersweet chocolate, finely chopped

Pastry cream

⅞ cup whole milk

1 vanilla bean, split lengthwise

2 egg yolks

⅓ cup sugar

1½ tablespoons cornstarch

To finish

2–3 tablespoons dark rum

confectioners' sugar, for dusting

a baking tray or jelly roll pan about 13 x 10 inches, greased and lined with parchment paper

wax paper

Makes 1 large cake

Using an electric standing mixer, electric hand mixer, or a rotary beater, beat the eggs, sugar, and vanilla vigorously for several minutes until very thick and mousse-like—when you lift the beaters out of the mixture, a thick ribbon-like trail should slowly fall back into the bowl.

Sift the flour and salt over the mixture, then gently fold in with a large, metal spoon. Pour the butter over the top and quickly fold in. Pour the mixture into the prepared tray or pan and spread out to a rectangle about ¼ inch thick. Bake in a preheated oven at 425°F for about 10 minutes until golden and just firm to the touch. Remove from the oven.

Meanwhile, cover a wire cooling rack with a dry cloth, then a sheet of parchment paper. Turn out the cooked sponge onto the prepared rack, then peel off the lining paper from the baking tray or pan. Using the cloth to help you, gently roll up the sponge from the narrow end, along with the parchment, to resemble a jelly roll. Don't worry if it cracks. Let cool, then wrap in wax paper for up to 24 hours or until ready to assemble.

To make the ganache, heat the cream in a medium saucepan until almost boiling. Remove from the heat, let cool for 1 minute, then tip in the chopped chocolate and stir gently until it has completely melted. Let cool, then beat vigorously until thick. If the mixture begins to separate, add 1 tablespoon chilled cream. Cover and keep at room temperature until ready to assemble, up to 3 hours.

To make the pastry cream, pour all but 2 tablespoons of the milk into a medium saucepan. Stir in the vanilla bean and heat gently until the milk is scalding hot but not actually boiling. Cover the pan and leave to infuse for 30 minutes–1 hour. Scrape as many seeds as possible from the bean into the milk, discard the bean, then reheat the milk. Put the egg yolks, the rest of the milk, sugar, and cornstarch in a bowl, stir until smooth, then pour the hot milk onto the mixture, stirring constantly. Pour the whole thing back into the pan

and stir constantly over medium heat until the mixture boils and thickens, about 2–3 minutes. Pour into a clean bowl, press a circle of damp, wax paper onto the surface, let cool, then chill until needed, up to 24 hours.

To assemble, unroll the sponge and peel off and discard the paper. Trim off any hard edges. Sprinkle with the rum, if using. Stir a quarter of the ganache into the pastry cream and spread over the sponge, leaving a 1-inch border of sponge all around. Roll up again, as for a jelly roll, then wrap tightly in foil to maintain the shape. Chill for 1 hour.

Unwrap, set on a cake board or platter and spread the rest of the ganache over the roll to cover completely. Run the back of a fork down the roll to resemble the ridges of the bark, then dip a sharp knife in hot water and cut off each end. Set these ends at one side or on top of the log to resemble sawn-off branches. Dust with confectioners' sugar "snow" and serve. The assembled log can be covered and kept in a cool place for up to 48 hours.

Nowadays, the French make this cake for Christmas, but its tradition harks back to the pagan Vikings. Their ceremony of the Yule log celebrated the sun at the time of the winter solstice. Yule was Odin, the father of the gods, and a massive log was burned in his honor to bring luck. These days, a small log is burned on Christmas Eve, accompanied by wine and songs, and is always lit by a piece saved from the previous year.

A plain sponge cake with a big difference—cardamom. Widely used in Scandinavia and South India, this attractive pale green spice with its tiny black seeds has a unique and memorable fragrance. This simple cake is also delicious topped with frosting.

chocolate, almond, and cardamom cake

7 oz. bittersweet chocolate, finely chopped

4 large eggs, separated

1 cup sugar

7 tablespoons unsalted butter, very soft

1 cup firmly packed ground almonds or 1¼ cups slivered almonds, finely ground in a blender

the ground black seeds from 4 cardamom pods

scant ⅔ cup all-purpose flour

¾ teaspoon baking powder

9-inch springform pan, greased and lined with parchment paper

Makes 1 medium cake

Put the chocolate into a large, heatproof bowl set over a saucepan of steaming but not boiling water. Leave until melted, stirring occasionally. Remove the bowl from the heat and leave until the chocolate feels just warm. Gently stir in the egg yolks, then the sugar. Work in the butter, then the ground almonds, ground cardamom, and flour.

Put the egg whites into a clean, dry, grease-free bowl and beat until stiff. Using a large metal spoon, fold the egg whites into the chocolate mixture in 3 batches.

Spoon into the prepared cake pan and bake in a preheated oven at 350°F for about 1 hour or until the mixture springs back when you press it gently with your finger.

Remove from the oven, carefully turn out onto a wire rack, and let cool. Wrap in foil, then leave overnight before cutting.

Serve dusted with confectioners' sugar or with whipped cream or ice cream. Best eaten within 5 days.

chocolate cherry cake

Better known as Black Forest Gâteau, I used this recipe as a pastry chef 25 years ago, and the chef who gave it to me has been using it since 1952!

9 large eggs, separated
1 cup sugar
1 cup unsweetened cocoa

Cream and cherry filling

25 oz. can Morello or Bing cherries in syrup, about 2⅓ cups

3 tablespoons Kirsch

scant 2 cups heavy cream

3 tablespoons sugar

2 oz. bittersweet chocolate, grated

three 8-inch layer cake pans, greased and lined with parchment paper

Makes 1 large cake

Put the egg yolks and sugar in a bowl and beat until thick and mousse-like—when the beaters are lifted, a ribbon-like trail will slowly fall back into the bowl. Sift the cocoa onto the mixture and gently fold in with a large metal spoon.

Put the egg whites into a spotlessly clean, grease-free bowl and beat with an electric mixer or hand mixer, until stiff peaks form. Carefully fold into the yolk mixture in 3 batches. Divide the mixture between the prepared pans, then bake in a preheated oven at 350°F for 20–25 minutes until the tops of the cakes spring back when you press it gently with your finger, and have shrunk away from the sides. Let cool in the pans before unmolding.

To make the filling, drain the cherries and save the syrup. Mix the Kirsch into the syrup. Leave the cherries on paper towels to drain. Reserve 12 to decorate.

Set one of the cooled sponges on a serving plate and sprinkle 2 tablespoons of the Kirsch syrup over the top.

Put the cream in a bowl and, using an electric mixer or hand mixer, whip until soft peaks form. Sprinkle the sugar over the cream and whip until slightly thicker. Reserve half the cream to cover the cake. Spread half the remaining cream over the bottom layer of sponge. Press half the cherries into the cream.

Sprinkle the second sponge layer with 2 tablespoons Kirsch syrup as before, then gently set on top of the first layer. Spread with cream and press in the cherries as before. Top with last layer of sponge. Sprinkle with 3 tablespoons Kirsch syrup. Pipe or spread the top and sides of the cake with the reserved cream, then decorate with the reserved cherries and grated chocolate. Chill until ready to serve. Best eaten within 48 hours.

Use the best quality chocolate to produce a good flavor. The sponge can be sprinkled with rum and a little rum can also be added to the dark mousse if you like.

chocolate roulade

6 large eggs, separated

1 cup firmly packed confectioners' sugar, sifted

a heaping ½ cup unsweetened cocoa

1–2 tablespoons rum (optional)

Dark mousse

7 oz. bittersweet chocolate, finely chopped

7 tablespoons unsalted butter, diced

4 large eggs, separated

1 tablespoon sugar

1–2 tablespoons rum (optional)

White mousse

1¼ cups heavy cream, chilled and whipped

3½ oz. best quality white chocolate, grated

To finish

grated dark and white chocolate or sifted confectioners' sugar and unsweetened cocoa

a 12- x 16½-inch baking tray, greased and lined with parchment paper

Makes 1 large cake

Put the egg yolks and ¾ cup of the confectioners' sugar in a bowl and beat until very light and mousse-like—the beaters should leave a ribbon-like trail when lifted out of the bowl. Sift the cocoa into the bowl and gently fold in with a large metal spoon. Put the egg whites in a bowl and beat until soft peaks form. Beat in the remaining confectioners' sugar, 1 tablespoon at a time, until stiff peaks form. Fold into the yolk mixture in 3 batches. Gently spread an even layer of mixture on the prepared tray, then bake in a preheated oven at 375°F for 8–10 minutes until firm to the touch.

Meanwhile, cover a wire cooling rack with a damp cloth topped with a sheet of parchment paper. Tip the cooked sponge onto the rack, then lift off the baking tray, peel the parchment off the bottom, and let cool.

To make the dark mousse, put the chocolate and butter in a heatproof bowl set over a saucepan of steaming not boiling water and melt gently. Remove from the heat and gently stir in the yolks, then the rum, if using. Let cool. Put the egg whites in a bowl, beat until stiff, then add the sugar and beat again until stiff. Fold into the chocolate mixture in 3 batches. Chill briefly until starting to set.

To make the white mousse, chill the whipped cream if necessary, then fold in the grated chocolate and chill until ready to assemble.

To assemble, sprinkle the sponge with rum, if using. Spread the dark mousse on top, leaving a ¾-inch border of sponge all around. Cover with white mousse, then roll up from the narrow end like a jelly roll, using the parchment paper to help you. Wrap in the parchment to give it a neat shape then chill for about 30 minutes–2 hours.

When ready to serve, remove the paper and transfer the roll to a serving plate. Decorate with grated chocolate or confectioners' sugar and cocoa.

Adding a touch of cocoa to the usual cracker crust gives an extra boost to this easy recipe.

chocolate chip cheesecake

Cracker crust

20 graham crackers, crushed

1 tablespoon unsweetened cocoa

scant ¼ cup sugar

5 tablespoons unsalted butter, melted

Chocolate filling

2¼ cups cream cheese

1 teaspoon vanilla extract

⅔ cup sugar

3 large eggs, lightly beaten

1 cup plus 1 tablespoon sour cream

3½ oz. bittersweet chocolate, finely chopped, or ⅔ cup chocolate chips

unsweetened cocoa, for dusting

a 9-inch springform pan, well greased

a baking sheet

Serves 8

To make the crust, put the cracker crumbs in a bowl, mix in the cocoa and sugar, then stir in the melted butter. Tip into the prepared pan and press firmly onto the base and halfway up the sides with the back of a spoon. Chill while making the filling.

Put the cream cheese, vanilla, and sugar into the bowl of an electric mixer and mix at low speed until very smooth. (You can also use a wooden spoon, but it's hard work.) Gradually beat in the eggs, increasing the speed as the mixture softens. Finally, beat in the sour cream. Using a large metal spoon, stir in the chopped chocolate.

Pour the filling into the crust, set the pan on the baking sheet, and bake in a preheated oven at 300°F for about 1¼ hours or until just firm. The cheesecake will probably sink as it cools, then crack, so turn off the oven and leave the door slightly ajar. Leave the cheesecake to cool slowly in the falling temperature for about 1 hour. Remove from the oven and let cool completely on a wire rack. Cover and chill overnight before unclipping the pan. Serve dusted with cocoa. Best eaten within 4 days—store well covered in the refrigerator.

¾ cup whole milk

2¼ oz. bittersweet chocolate, finely chopped

scant ⅔ cup sugar

4 tablespoons unsalted butter, at room temperature

½ teaspoon vanilla extract

1 large egg, beaten

1¼ cups all-purpose flour

1½ teaspoons baking powder

Chocolate frosting

3½ oz. bittersweet chocolate, finely chopped

1 tablespoon corn syrup

2 tablespoons unsalted butter, at room temperature

12-cup regular muffin pan, lined with paper liners

Makes 12

Put the milk in a saucepan and heat until scalding hot but not boiling. Put the chocolate into a bowl, add about one-third of the sugar, then pour over the hot milk and stir until smooth and melted. Let cool.

Put the butter in a bowl, add the vanilla and remaining sugar. Using an electric mixer or wooden spoon, beat until light and fluffy, then gradually beat in the egg. Working in batches, stir in the chocolate mixture alternately with the flour. Mix well to make a smooth, thick batter. Pour or spoon into the paper cake cases until half full.

Bake in a preheated oven at 350°F for 15–18 minutes or until well risen, and the cakes spring back when gently pressed with your finger. Remove from the oven and let cool on a wire rack.

To make the chocolate frosting, which can be used for large sponge cakes as well as small cupcakes and fairy cakes, put the chocolate in the top of a double boiler, or in a heatproof bowl set over a saucepan of steaming but not boiling water, and melt gently. Remove the bowl from the pan and stir in the syrup and butter. When smooth, let cool, stirring occasionally. When very thick and on the point of setting, dip the top of each little cake into the chocolate frosting (or spread it on) until thickly coated. Let set until firm. Best eaten within 3 days.

old-fashioned cupcakes

These individual cakes, with a light moist crumb and fudgy topping, were the after-school snack for generations of deserving children. There are two stories about how they got their name. The first is that they were baked in cups. The second theory is that it came from the original recipe measurements; four cups flour, three cups sugar, and one of melted butter—this recipe is slightly smaller!

chocolate chip banana muffins

2 ripe, medium bananas

1 stick unsalted butter, at room temperature

½ cup light brown sugar

1 large egg, beaten

½ cup walnut pieces

1¾ oz. bittersweet chocolate, coarsely chopped, or ⅓ cup chocolate chips

1⅔ cups all-purpose flour

2 teaspoons bakig powder

12-cup deep muffin pan, lined with paper liners

Makes 12

Mash the bananas with a fork (they should not be too smooth) and set aside. Put the butter in a bowl and, using an electric mixer or wooden spoon, beat until creamy, then beat in the sugar. When the mixture is light and fluffy, gradually beat in the egg.

Using a large metal spoon, stir in the bananas, nuts, and chocolate or chocolate chips. Add the flour and gently fold in to make a coarse-looking mixture: to avoid a tough end result, try to use as few movements as possible. Spoon into the prepared muffin pan to three-quarters full and bake immediately in a preheated oven at 400°F for 15–20 minutes until golden brown, well risen, and firm to the touch. Let cool for a minute then gently unmold, using a round-bladed knife to loosen the muffins. Cool on a wire rack and eat while still warm, or the same day.

chocolate chip muffins

Sift the flour with the cocoa, baking powder, baking soda, and salt into a bowl. Set aside. Put the butter in a bowl and, using an electric mixer or wooden spoon, beat until creamy, then gradually beat in the eggs and vanilla extract. When the mixture is light and fluffy, stir in the sour cream, then 3½ oz of the chocolate or ⅔ cup of the chocolate chips, until well mixed. Add the flour mixture and stir briefly until barely mixed.

Spoon into the prepared muffin pan to three-quarters full, sprinkle with the remaining chocolate or chocolate chips and bake in the preheated oven at 400°F for 20–25 minutes until firm to the touch. Let cool for a minute then carefully unmold and cool on a wire rack. Eat while still warm or the same day.

1¾ cups all-purpose flour

½ cup unsweetened cocoa

1 teaspoon baking powder

1 teaspoon baking soda

a pinch of salt

1 stick unsalted butter, at room temperature

½ cup firmly packed sugar

½ teaspoon vanilla extract

2 large eggs, lightly beaten

1 cup sour cream

5¼ oz. bittersweet chocolate, coarsely chopped, or 1 cup chocolate chips

12-cup deep muffin pan, lined with paper liners

Makes 12

Eaten warm for breakfast all over America, muffins should have a coarser crumb than cupcakes and a more robust, less sweet taste.

Two shortbread doughs—one vanilla, one chocolate—are rolled together, then sliced into spectacular cookies. For the best taste, only butter will do—and the traditional ground rice adds the authentic grainy texture.

pinwheel cookies

Put the butter in a bowl and, using an electric mixer or a wooden spoon, beat until creamy, then gradually beat in the sugar. Continue beating until the mixture becomes light and fluffy, then beat in the vanilla.

Put half of the mixture into another bowl. Sift the ground rice, rice flour, or cornstarch, and half the flour onto one mixture, then sift the remaining flour and the cocoa onto the other mixture. Work each mixture using a wooden spoon or your hands to make a stiff dough. In hot weather, wrap each piece of dough in wax paper and chill until firm.

Set the plain dough in the middle of a sheet of wax paper and, using a well-floured rolling pin, roll out to a rectangle about 8½ x 11 inches. Roll out the chocolate dough on a second sheet of paper in the same way, then gently invert the chocolate dough on top of the plain dough. Neaten the edges with your hands, then very carefully roll it up, starting from one long side, rather like a jelly roll. Don't worry if cracks appear—just press them together with your fingers. Wrap the roll in wax paper and chill for 15 minutes or until very firm.

Using a long, sharp knife, cut the roll into ½-inch thick slices. Arrange slightly apart on the prepared baking sheets, then bake in a preheated oven at 350°F for 12–15 minutes until firm and slightly golden at the edges. Cool for a couple of minutes until firm, then transfer to a wire rack to cool. When completely cold, store in an airtight container. Eat within 1 week or freeze for up to 1 month.

Note Ground rice is available in natural food stores and near the baby food section of supermarkets. An alternative is very fine semolina.

2 sticks plus 5 tablespoons unsalted butter, at room temperature

¾ cup sugar

½ teaspoon vanilla extract

2¾ cups all-purpose flour

scant ¼ cup ground rice, rice flour, or cornstarch

a heaping ¼ cup unsweetened cocoa, sifted

several baking sheets, greased

Makes 28

These cookies were first made (without chocolate) in medieval German monasteries. The most famous come from Nüremburg, a center of the spice trade in the 16th century, when chocolate first arrived in Europe. One snowy December, I visited a small bakery working around the clock to make enough for the Advent Market. The baker told me that the recipe differs from other German ones in that it is based on meringue, as many as seven spices, and nuts rather than honey and flour.

lebkuchen

¾ cup unblanched almonds (with brown skins left on)

1 oz. bittersweet chocolate, coarsely chopped

2 tablespoons very finely chopped mixed peel or 1 tablespoon each chopped candied lemon peel and orange peel

½ teaspoon ground cinnamon

½ teaspoon ground ginger

¼ teaspoon grated nutmeg

¼ teaspoon ground black pepper

¼ teaspoon ground cloves

¼ teaspoon ground allspice

2 large egg whites

⅞ cup confectioners' sugar, sifted

Chocolate glaze

3½ oz. bittersweet chocolate, finely chopped

¾ cup firm-packed confectioners' sugar, sifted

several baking sheets, lined with parchment paper

Makes 12

Put the almonds and chocolate into a food processor and work until finely ground. Thoroughly mix with the mixed peel and spices.

Put the egg whites in a spotlessly clean bowl and, using an electric mixer or electric hand mixer, beat until stiff peaks form. Gradually beat in the confectioners' sugar, then beat for a further minute or so to make a very thick, glossy meringue. Add the ground almond and chocolate mixture and carefully fold in with a large metal spoon.

Put tablespoon-sized mounds of the mixture on the prepared baking sheets, setting them well apart, then spread each into a neat circle about 3½ inches in diameter. If you're feeling creative you can make heart shapes with the mixture.

Bake in a preheated oven at 325°F for 15–20 minutes until the cookies are pale gold. Let cool, then peel off the parchment.

Meanwhile, to make the chocolate glaze, put the chocolate in a bowl, set it over a saucepan of steaming water, and melt gently. Remove and cool. Mix the sifted confectioners' sugar with 4 tablespoons hot water to make a smooth glacé frosting, then stir in the chocolate to make a fairly runny mixture—if necessary, stir in a little extra warm water. Dip each cookie in the glaze to coat thinly, then leave to set on waxed paper. Store in an airtight container. Eat within 1 week.

speckled cookies

Using an electric mixer, balloon whisk, or a wooden spoon, beat the butter until creamy. Add the confectioners' sugar and beat, slowly at first, until light and fluffy. Beat in the vanilla extract, then stir in the oats.

Sift the flour, salt, and baking powder into the bowl and mix with a wooden spoon or your hands to make a stiff dough.

Shape the dough into a log about 3 inches in diameter, then wrap in wax paper and chill for 20 minutes until firm.

Slice the log into rounds about ¼ inch thick. Grate the chocolate and sprinkle about 1 teaspoon on the top of each round. Set the rounds slightly apart on the prepared sheet. Bake in a preheated oven at 325°F for 20 minutes until lightly golden around the edges. Leave the cookies on the sheet for a couple of minutes to firm up, then transfer to a wire cooling rack to cool completely. Store in an airtight container. Eat within 5 days or freeze for up to 1 month.

1¾ sticks unsalted butter, at room temperature

¾ cup confectioners' sugar, sifted

1 teaspoon vanilla extract

¾ cup rolled oats

1⅓ cups all-purpose flour

a pinch of salt

½ teaspoon baking powder

1½ oz. bittersweet chocolate, chilled

several baking sheets, greased

Makes 20

Wonderfully easy, attractive cookies that manage the impossible: they crumble in the hand, then melt in the mouth.

chocolate maple pecan cookies

Put the butter in a bowl and, using an electric mixer or wooden spoon, beat until creamy. Beat in the sugar and maple syrup until light and fluffy. Gradually beat in the egg then, using your hands or a wooden spoon, work in the flour, chocolate, and nuts to make a rather soft dough. Using well-floured hands, shape the dough into a log 9 x 2 inches thick. Wrap in wax paper and chill overnight or for 2 hours in the freezer (the uncooked dough can be stored in the refrigerator for up to 5 days or up to 1 month in the freezer).

Unwrap the dough, cut into ¼-inch slices, then arrange well apart on the prepared trays. Bake in a preheated oven at 400°F for 10–12 minutes until pale gold. Leave on the sheets for a few minutes to firm up then transfer to wire racks to cool. Store in an airtight container and eat within 1 week or freeze for up to 1 month.

1½ sticks unsalted butter, at room temperature

a heaping ¾ cup light brown sugar

2 tablespoons maple syrup

1 medium egg, lightly beaten

2 cups all-purpose flour

2 teaspoons baking powder

1¾ oz. bittersweet chocolate, coarsely chopped, or ⅓ cup chocolate chips

½ cup pecan nuts, chopped

several baking sheets, well greased

Makes 36

chocolate pecan chunkies

7 oz. bittersweet chocolate, chopped

4 tablespoons unsalted butter, at room temperature

2 large eggs, at room temperature

⅔ cup sugar

½ teaspoon vanilla extract

3 tablespoons all-purpose flour

¼ teaspoon baking powder

3½ oz. bittersweet or white chocolate, chopped, or ⅔ cup chocolate chips

⅞ cup pecan or walnut pieces

several baking sheets, greased and lined

Makes 22

Put the chocolate in a heatproof bowl set over a saucepan of steaming but not boiling water and melt gently. Remove the bowl, stir in the butter, and let cool.

Put the eggs, sugar, and vanilla in a large bowl and, using an electric mixer or rotary beater, beat until very thick and mousse-like. When you lift the beaters, a thick, ribbon-like trail should fall back into the bowl.

Sift the flour into the mixture and carefully fold in with a large metal spoon. Gently fold in the chocolate mixture, then the chopped chocolate or chocolate chips and nuts. Put tablespoon-sized mounds of the mixture onto the prepared baking sheets, setting well apart, because the mixture spreads. Bake in a preheated oven at 350°F for about 10 minutes until barely set. Let cool and firm up on the trays, then transfer to wire cooling racks. Store an airtight container and eat within 1 week or freeze for up to 1 month.

soft and fudgy brownies

This is my mother-in-law's recipe for very soft and fudgy brownies. The original recipe comes from a dog-eared newspaper clipping, circa 1950, of recipes for Church bakes sales. Over the years, the sugar has been reduced and the nuts omitted altogether to please her grandchildren, but she insists on slight undercooking to get the right, gooey texture.

1 stick unsalted butter, at room temperature

1½ cups sugar

5 large eggs, lightly beaten

1 teaspoon vanilla extract

⅔ cup all-purpose flour

¾ cup unsweetened cocoa powder

8 oz. bittersweet chocolate, melted and cooled

12- x 7½-inch cake pan, greased and lined with parchment paper

Makes 30

Put the butter and sugar in a bowl and beat until soft and fluffy, then beat in the vanilla. Gradually beat in the eggs, a little at a time. Sift the flour with cocoa into the bowl and stir well. Lastly, mix in the melted chocolate. Spoon into the prepared pan and spread evenly.

Bake in a preheated oven at 325°F for about 20 minutes until almost firm to the touch. Let cool, then cut into tiny squares and remove from the pan. Store in lidded container and eat within 3 days.

Best eaten warm with vanilla ice cream.

chocolate desserts

chocolate chunk crunch ice cream

Mix the breadcrumbs with the brown sugar and spread over the base of the baking pan. Bake in a preheated oven at 400°C, stirring frequently, for about 10–15 minutes until the mixture is a dark golden brown. Let cool completely, then break up the lumps and mix with the chopped chocolate.

Put the cream in a bowl and, using an electric mixer or beater, whip until it stands in soft peaks. Beat in the vanilla and sugar. Spoon into an ice cream maker and freeze until slushy and almost frozen. Alternatively, spoon into a freezer-proof container, then freeze and stir every 10 minutes or so until slushy.

Stir in the chocolate mixture and freeze again until firm. If not using immediately, transfer the ice cream to a suitable lidded container and store in the freezer for up to 1 week. Serve with one of the hot chocolate sauces (page 56–7).

1¾ cups loose-packed whole-wheat breadcrumbs

⅔ cup lightly packed light brown sugar

3 oz. bittersweet chocolate, finely chopped

1¼ cups heavy cream, well chilled

1 teaspoon vanilla extract

1½ tablespoons sugar

a baking pan, any size, lightly oiled

ice cream maker (optional)

Serves 4–6

chocolate spice ice

7 oz. bittersweet chocolate, finely chopped

1¼ cups milk

1 cinnamon stick or ½ teaspoon ground cinnamon

3 large egg yolks

a heaped ⅓ cup sugar

⅞ cup heavy cream, well chilled

ice cream maker (optional)

Serves 4–6

Put the chopped chocolate into a large, heatproof bowl.

Put the milk and the cinnamon stick or ground cinnamon in a saucepan, heat until almost boiling, then cover the pan and leave to infuse for 15 minutes.

Put the egg yolks and sugar in a heatproof bowl and stir well. Gently reheat the milk, remove the cinnamon stick, then pour the hot milk onto the egg mixture, stirring constantly. When well mixed, pour the mixture back into the saucepan. Stir gently over low heat until the mixture thickens into a custard—don't let it boil or it will curdle. Remove from the heat, then pour the custard over the chopped chocolate and stir gently until smooth. Let cool, then cover and chill.

Whip the cream until it forms soft peaks, then fold in the cold chocolate mixture. Pour into an ice cream maker and churn until frozen. Eat immediately or store in the freezer. Alternatively, freeze in a freezer-proof container, stirring occasionally.

easy chocolate mousse

This classic French recipe has been going strong for many generations; my mother learned to make it when she lived in Paris in the 1930s. It can easily be halved or doubled and served in a large bowl, or in individual cups, glasses, or dishes, with crisp tuiles.

Put the chocolate and water, coffee, brandy, or rum into a heatproof bowl set over a saucepan of steaming but not boiling water and melt very gently, taking care not to overheat the chocolate.

Remove from the heat and gently stir in the butter. Let cool for 1 minute, then gently stir in the yolks, one at a time.

Put the whites into a spotlessly clean, grease-free bowl and, using an electric mixer or a balloon whisk, beat until stiff peaks form. Mix about 1 tablespoon into the chocolate mixture to soften it. Fold in the rest of the whites in 3 batches using a large metal spoon until just combined—do not overmix.

Carefully spoon into a serving bowl or individual dishes; you can serve coffee-flavored chocolate mousse in tiny cups set on saucers, or—for mousse made with alcohol—use brandy or champagne or pretty crystal glasses. This mousse is very rich. Chill for at least 2 hours before serving. Best eaten within 12 hours.

4½ oz. bittersweet chocolate, finely chopped

2 tablespoons water, strong black coffee, brandy or rum

1 tablespoon unsalted butter, at room temperature

4 large eggs, separated

a glass bowl, coffee cups, brandy glasses, champagne flutes, or sundae dishes

Serves 4–6

If you've never tried your hand at a steamed pudding, try this one—comfort food at its very best. The mixture is classic chocolate sponge but with ground almonds for a richer flavor. Steaming makes the texture light-as-a-feather, a once-eaten never-forgotten treat. Serve with a sauce from pages 56–57 (I think the custard is best).

Pour water into a large saucepan until about one-third full. Put an old saucer upside-down in the pan, then bring to a boil, ready to cook the pudding. You can also use a steamer.

Put the butter in a bowl and, using an electric mixer or a wooden spoon, beat until creamy. Add the sugar and beat until the mixture is very light and fluffy. Gradually beat in the eggs, beating well after each addition. Sift the flour with the baking powder, almonds, and cocoa then, using a large metal spoon, fold it into the beaten mixture with the milk. Spoon the mixture into the prepared basin, about two-thirds full. Cut a large square of foil, and butter one side. Fold the foil down the middle to make a large pleat (to let the pudding expand), then put the foil over the top of the bowl, buttered side down.

Tie the foil tightly around the top of the bowl with kitchen twine (make a twine handle too if possible), then set the bowl onto the saucer in the saucepan— the water should come half way up the sides of the bowl, so pour out any excess water or top up with extra boiling water. Cover the pan and boil the pudding steadily for about 1½ hours until firm, topping up the water from time to time to prevent the pan boiling dry.

Remove from the saucepan and carefully remove the foil. Loosen the pudding with a round-bladed knife, turn out onto a warmed plate, and serve with custard.

1 stick unsalted butter, at room temperature

a heaping ½ cup sugar

2 large eggs, lightly beaten

scant ¾ cup all-purpose flour

1 teaspoon baking powder

⅓ cup ground almonds or ½ cup slivered almonds, ground in a blender

2 tablespoons unsweetened cocoa

1 tablespoon milk

chocolate custard (page 57), to serve

a heatproof ceramic bowl, about 32 fl. oz., well buttered

a large sheet of foil

Serves 6

steamed chocolate pudding
with hot chocolate custard

upside-down pear cake

3½ oz. bittersweet chocolate, finely chopped

7 tablespoons unsalted butter, at room temperature

⅔ cup firmly packed light brown sugar, sifted

2 large eggs, beaten

3 pieces preserved ginger in syrup, finely chopped, plus 3 tablespoons syrup from the jar

scant 1 cup all-purpose flour

1½ teaspoons baking powder

Pear topping

3 tablespoons unsalted butter

¼ cup light brown sugar

2 large or 3 small pears, peeled, cored, and quartered

9-inch sauté pan or cake pan (not springform), greased

Serves 8

To make the pear topping, put the butter in a small saucepan, heat until melted, then stir in the sugar. When smooth and the sugar has dissolved, pour the mixture into the base of the pan. Arrange the pears, rounded side down, on top of the mixture.

Put the chocolate in a heatproof bowl set over a saucepan of steaming but not boiling water. Melt very gently. Remove and let cool while making the batter.

Put the butter in a bowl and, using an electric mixer or wooden spoon, beat until creamy. Beat in the sugar. Continue beating until fluffy, then gradually beat in the eggs, followed by the chopped ginger, ginger syrup, and the melted chocolate. Fold in the flour with a large metal spoon and, when well mixed, spread the batter on top of the fruit in the pan and level the surface.

Bake in a preheated oven at 350°F for 45–60 minutes until firm to the touch, then turn out onto a warmed serving plate to reveal the sticky pear topping. Serve warm with ice cream or whipped cream, a chocolate sauce, or chocolate custard (pages 56–57). It can also be left to cool and eaten as a cake.

A good dessert for a winter Sunday lunch—pears and chocolate make one of the happiest combinations.

Pavlova

3 large egg whites

a pinch of salt

1⅛ cups firmly packed light brown sugar, sifted

1 teaspoon cornstarch

½ teaspoon vanilla extract

1 teaspoon white vinegar

Chocolate-chestnut topping

1¼ cups heavy cream, well chilled

2 tablespoons sugar

2 tablespoons dark rum (optional)

3½ oz. bittersweet chocolate, grated

14 oz. can chestnuts in syrup, drained

a baking sheet lined with parchment paper

Serves 6

To make the pavlova, put the egg whites and salt into a spotlessly clean, grease-free bowl and beat with an electric mixer or balloon whisk, until they form stiff peaks. Gradually beat in half of the sugar, the cornstarch, and vanilla to make a stiff meringue. Using a large metal spoon, gently fold in the rest of the sugar—don't overwork, or the mixture will turn sticky.

Spoon the mixture onto the prepared baking sheet to make a circle about 9 inches diameter and 1¼ inches deep. Make a shallow dip in the middle.

Bake in a preheated oven at 300°F for 1–1¼ hours until very crisp on the outside and slightly soft in the middle. Turn off the oven and leave the pavlova to cool inside. Remove from the oven, peel away the parchment paper, and set the pavlova on a large serving plate. Don't worry if any cracks form.

To make the topping, put the cream in a large bowl and beat with an electric mixer or balloon whisk, until it stands in soft peaks. Beat in the sugar and rum, if using, and beat until almost stiff. Carefully fold in half the chocolate and all the chestnuts.

Pile the mixture on top of the pavlova, then sprinkle with the remaining chocolate. Serve immediately or chill and serve the same day with chocolate sauce.

chocolate pavlova
with chocolate and chestnuts

A combination of crunchy and sticky meringue plus whipped cream, grated chocolate, and sweet chestnuts makes a special holiday-time pudding. Serve with the Rich Dark Chocolate Sauce on page 56.

warm chocolate torte

Not a pudding, or a cake, or even a mousse, this flourless concoction defies categorization—but is easy to achieve. Eat it warm with plenty of vanilla ice cream and beautiful fresh berries, such as raspberries or blueberries.

Put the chocolate in a heatproof bowl set over a saucepan of steaming but not boiling water and let it melt gently. Remove the bowl from the pan, stir the chocolate gently until smooth, then set aside. Alternatively, use a double-boiler.

Put the butter into a bowl and, using an electric mixer, balloon whisk, or wooden spoon, beat until creamy. Add the sugar and beat until light and fluffy. Beat in the egg yolks, one at a time, beating well after each addition. Beat in the cooled chocolate and the vanilla or coffee. Using a large metal spoon, stir in the ground almonds.

Put the egg whites and salt in a spotlessly clean, grease-free bowl and, using a balloon whisk or an electric mixer, beat until they form soft peaks.

Using a large metal spoon, gently fold the egg whites into the chocolate mixture in 3 batches. Spoon the mixture into the prepared cake pan and bake in a preheated oven at 400°F for 10 minutes. Then reduce the oven temperature to 350°F and bake for a further 7–10 minutes until barely set—do not overcook or the torte will be dry.

Remove from the oven and set the pan on a wet cloth. Do not unmold the cake, but run a round-bladed knife around the side of the pan to loosen the cake. Leave for 10–15 minutes, then gently unmold, dust with confectioners' sugar, and serve warm, with whipped cream and raspberries or with vanilla ice cream. Alternatively, leave until completely cold, then unmold and wrap in foil. Store at room temperature for up to 48 hours, then gently warm before serving.

4½ oz. bittersweet chocolate, finely chopped

1 stick unsalted butter, at room temperature

a heaping ⅛ cup sugar

4 large eggs, separated

½ teaspoon vanilla extract or 1 tablespoon extra strong (espresso) coffee

1 cup firmly packed ground almonds, or 1¼ cups slivered almonds, ground in a blender

a pinch of salt

confectioners' sugar, for dusting

8-inch springform pan, greased and lined with parchment paper

Serves 6–8

chocolate sauces

rich dark chocolate sauce

To make a creamy variation of this sauce, use light cream instead of the water or, for a flavored sauce, use a tablespoon or so of brandy, rum, or coffee liqueur instead of some of the water.

3½ oz. bittersweet chocolate, finely chopped

4 tablespoons unsalted butter, diced

Serves 4–6

Put the chopped chocolate, butter, and scant ½ cup water in a heatproof bowl set over a saucepan of steaming not boiling water. Stir frequently until melted and very smooth. Remove from the heat and stir well until glossy and slightly thickened. As the sauce cools it will become even thicker. Serve warm.

creamy chocolate sauce

A very quick, rich sauce for ice cream, profiteroles, and steamed puddings. Just before serving, it can be flavored with rum, brandy, or coffee liqueur to taste. For a slightly thinner and less rich sauce use single cream, or cream mixed half and half with milk or coffee.

Put the cream into a small, heavy saucepan and heat gently, stirring frequently. When the cream comes to a boil, remove the pan from the heat, let cool for a minute, then stir in the chopped chocolate. Stir gently until the sauce is smooth. Stir in the vanilla and serve immediately.

1 cup heavy cream

3 oz. bittersweet chocolate, finely chopped

½ teaspoon vanilla extract

Serves 4–6

chocolate custard

The classic sauce for steamed puddings.

2 cups whole milk

3 tablespoons unsweetened cocoa powder

scant ⅓ cup sugar

1 tablespoon cornstarch

2 egg yolks

Serves 4–6

Put all but 2 tablespoons of the milk in a large saucepan and heat until almost boiling. Sift the cocoa, sugar, and cornstarch into a heatproof bowl, stir in the egg yolks and milk to make a thick paste, then stir in the hot milk. Strain the mixture back into the saucepan and stir constantly over low heat until the mixture thickens—don't let the mixture boil or it will separate.

Remove the custard from the heat and use at once, or keep it warm until ready to serve.

white chocolate sauce

The flavor depends on the quality of the chocolate, so use the best you can lay your hands on rather than children's bars.

Put the chocolate in a heatproof bowl set over a saucepan of steaming but not boiling water and melt gently. Remove the bowl from the heat and stir gently until smooth.

Put the cream and milk in a saucepan and heat until scalding hot, but not quite boiling. Remove from the heat. Pour onto the chocolate in a thin stream, beating the mixture constantly, to make a smooth sauce. Pour into a warmed pitcher and serve at once with desserts, especially ice cream, or let cool and serve with red berries or Warm Chocolate Torte (page 52)

7½ oz. good-quality white chocolate, finely chopped

⅞ cup heavy cream

⅛ cup whole milk

Serves 4–6

chocolate drinks

Don't wait for snow! Have this hot chocolate any time.

the best hot chocolate

3 oz. bittersweet chocolate, broken into pieces

1 tablespoon sugar, or to taste

1 vanilla bean, split lengthwise

1¼ cups whole milk

scant ⅓ cup whipping or heavy cream, whipped

grated chocolate or unsweetened cocoa, for sprinkling

Serves 2

Put the chocolate pieces, sugar, vanilla, and milk into a small, heavy saucepan. Heat gently, stirring, until the chocolate has melted, then bring to a boil, beating constantly until very smooth and frothy. Remove the vanilla bean. Pour into warmed mugs, top with whipped cream and a sprinkling of chocolate or cocoa, then serve.

3½ oz. bittersweet chocolate, broken into pieces

2 cups whole milk

2 tablespoons vodka

scant ⅓ cup whipping or heavy cream, whipped (optional)

grated chocolate or cocoa, for sprinkling

Serves 2

Put the chocolate and half the milk into a small, heavy saucepan and heat gently, stirring constantly, until melted. Add the rest of the milk and heat, stirring frequently, until piping hot and smoothly blended. Pour into warmed mugs, add the vodka, then top with the whipped cream, if using, and the grated chocolate or cocoa. Drink very hot.

Not one to share with the kids.

hot russian

hot spanish

Dip long cinnamon sticks in melted chocolate, let set, then use as stirring spoons for this traditional drink.

1¾ oz. bittersweet chocolate, broken into pieces

1 cup whole milk

1 tablespoon sugar

1 cinnamon stick

1¼ cups hot, strong black coffee

2 tablespoons brandy (optional)

4 curls of fresh orange peel

Serves 4

Put the chocolate, milk, sugar, and cinnamon stick in a saucepan and heat gently, stirring constantly, until smooth and melted. Bring to a boil, beating, then remove from the heat and beat in the coffee and brandy, if using. Remove the cinnamon stick. Put the orange peel into tall, warmed, heatproof glasses and pour over the hot mixture.

3½ oz. bittersweet chocolate, broken into pieces

1 tablespoon sugar, or to taste

1¼ cups whole milk

2 cups freshly made, hot, strong black coffee

scant ⅛ cup whipping or heavy cream, whipped

Serves 4

Put the chocolate, sugar, and milk into a heavy saucepan and stir over a low heat until melted and smooth. Bring to a boil, beating constantly, then remove from the heat and beat in the fresh, hot coffee. Pour into warmed mugs and top with whipped cream.

The classic chocolate-coffee combo.

hot mocha

iced mocha

A chilled-down version of Hot Mocha (page 61) using ice cream and ice cubes instead of whipped cream.

3½ oz. bittersweet chocolate, broken into pieces

1 tablespoon sugar, or to taste

1¼ cups whole milk

2 cups freshly made hot, strong black coffee

4 scoops vanilla ice cream (optional)

ice cubes, to serve

Serves 4

Put the chocolate, sugar, and milk into a heavy saucepan and stir over low heat until melted and smooth. Bring to a boil, beating constantly. Remove from the heat and beat in the freshly made hot coffee. Let cool, then chill. Put in a blender, add the ice cream, if using, then blend until smooth. Fill tall, chilled glasses with ice cubes, then pour over the mocha drink and serve.

my chocolate milkshake

Chocolate is everyone's favorite milkshake. In my version, the ice cubes make it lightly frothy.

Put the milk, drinking chocolate, and ice cubes into a blender and pulse briefly until smooth. Put a scoop of ice cream into each of 4 chilled tall glasses. Pour over the milkshake, sprinkle with a little grated chocolate or sprinkles, and serve with straws.

3 cups whole milk, well chilled

6 tablespoons drinking chocolate powder

6 ice cubes

4 scoops chocolate ice cream, about 3½ oz.

grated chocolate or chocolate sprinkles, to serve

Serves 4

index

büche de noël—yule log, 18

cakes:
chocolate, almond, and
cardamom cake, 21
chocolate cherry cake, 22
chocolate chip
cheesecake, 26
chocolate roulade, 25
old fashioned cupcakes,
29
chocolate confections,
16–41
chocolate drinks, 58–63
best hot chocolate, 60
chocolate milkshake, 63
iced mocha, 63
hot mocha, 61
hot Russian, 60
hot Spanish, 61
chocolate puddings, 42–53
chocolate sauces, 54–57
chocolate custard, 57
creamy chocolate sauce,
56
rich dark chocolate sauce,
56
white chocolate sauce, 57
choosing chocolate, 8
chopping chocolate, 8
Christmas prunes, 12

cookies:
chocolate maple pecan, 38
chocolate pecan chunkies,
38
lebkuchen, 34
pinwheel, 33
soft and fudgy brownies, 41
speckled cookies, 36
cupcakes, old fashioned, 29

easy chocolate mousse, 45

fudge:
chocolate and cream, 15
nut, 15

ice cream:
chocolate chunk crunch
ice cream, 44
chocolate spice ice, 44

melting chocolate, 8
microwaving chocolate, 8
mousse, easy chocolate, 45
muffins:
chocolate chip banana, 30
chocolate chip, 30

nut fudge, 15
pavlova, chocolate, with and
chestnuts, 51

pear, upside-down pear
cake, 49
pinwheel cookies, 33
prunes, Christmas, 12
pudding:
hot chocolate, 46
upside-down pear cake,
49

steamed chocolate pudding,
46
storing chocolate, 8
sweet treats, 10–15

torte, warm chocolate, 52
truffles:
cherry liqueur, 13
chocolate, 13
Drambuie or Tia Maria, 13
rum or brandy, 13
snowball, 13

upside down pear pudding,
48

warm chocolate torte, 52
white chocolate:
sauce, 57
snowball truffles, 13

yule log, 18

conversion charts

Weights and measures have been rounded up
or down slightly to make measuring easier.

Volume equivalents:

American	Metric	Imperial
1 teaspoon	5 ml	
1 tablespoon	15 ml	
¼ cup	60 ml	2 fl.oz.
⅓ cup	75 ml	2½ fl.oz.
½ cup	125 ml	4 fl.oz.
⅔ cup	150 ml	5 fl.oz. (¼ pint)
¾ cup	175 ml	6 fl.oz.
1 cup	250 ml	8 fl.oz.

Weight equivalents: Measurements:

Imperial	Metric	Inches	Cm
1 oz.	25 g	¼ inch	5 mm
2 oz.	50 g	½ inch	1 cm
3 oz.	75 g	¾ inch	1.5 cm
4 oz.	125 g	1 inch	2.5 cm
5 oz.	150 g	2 inches	5 cm
6 oz.	175 g	3 inches	7 cm
7 oz.	200 g	4 inches	10 cm
8 oz. (½ lb.)	250 g	5 inches	12 cm
9 oz.	275 g	6 inches	15 cm
10 oz.	300 g	7 inches	18 cm
11 oz.	325 g	8 inches	20 cm
12 oz.	375 g	9 inches	23 cm
13 oz.	400 g	10 inches	25 cm
14 oz.	425 g	11 inches	28 cm
15 oz.	475 g	12 inches	30 cm
16 oz. (1 lb.)	500 g		
2 1b.	1 kg		

Oven temperatures:

110°C	(225°F)	Gas ¼
120°C	(250°F)	Gas ½
140°C	(275°F)	Gas 1
150°C	(300°F)	Gas 2
160°C	(325°F)	Gas 3
180°C	(350°F)	Gas 4
190°C	(375°F)	Gas 5
200°C	(400°F)	Gas 6
220°C	(425°F)	Gas 7
230°C	(450°F)	Gas 8
240°C	(475°F)	Gas 9